Counting From 1 To 10

I'm going to teach you how to count from one to ten,
and when we're through we will sing a counting song.

one .... uno
two ....dos
three .... tres
four...cuatro
five ....cinco
six.. seis
seven .... siete
eight ....ocho
nine...nueve
ten ....diez

Good! Now, let's say the numbers one more time.

one .... uno
two ....dos
three .... tres
four...cuatro
five ....cinco
six.. seis
seven .... siete
eight ....ocho
nine...nueve
ten ....diez

Oh, I can count from one to ten, one to ten, one to ten.
I can count from one to ten, listen to me.

Uno, dos, tres, cuatro, cinco, seis, siete, ocho, nueve, y diez.
I can count from one to ten, listen to me.

(Repeat)

Counting from 1 to 10

Match the number word to the correct picture.

dos

cuatro

tres

seis

ocho

diez

cinco

nueve

uno

siete

The Hello Song

(Chorus 1:)
Hello, hello, hello to you.
I wish to say, I wish to say hello to you.
Hola, hola, hola a ti.
Quiero decir, quiero decir hola a ti.

Hello. How are you? ....Hola. ¿Cómo estás?
I am good. ....Estoy bien.
Hola. ¿Cómo estás? ....Hello. How are you?
Estoy más o menos. ....I am so-so.

(Chorus 2:)
Hola, hola, hola a ti.
Quiero decir, quiero decir hola a ti.
Hello, hello, hello to you.
I wish to say, I wish to say hello to you.

What is your name? ....¿Cómo te llamas?
My name is Roberto. ....Me llamo Roberto.
¿Cómo te llamas? ....What is your name?
Me llamo Marta. ....My name is Marta.
(Chorus 1)

Are you in school? ....¿Estás en la escuela?
Yes, I am in school. ....Sí, estoy en la escuela.
¿Qué aprendes? ....What are you learning?
Aprendo idiomas distintos. ....I am learning different languages.
(Chorus 2)

It was nice to speak with you. ...Fue agradable hablar contigo.
Goodbye, Roberto, see you tomorrow. ..Adiós, Roberto, hasta mañana.
Fue agradable hablar contigo. ...It was nice to speak with you.
Adiós, Marta, hasta luego. ....Goodbye, Marta, see you later.

(Chorus 3:)
Goodbye, goodbye, goodbye to you.
I wish to say, I wish to say goodbye to you.
Adiós, adiós, adiós a ti.
Quiero decir, quiero decir adiós a ti.

¡Adiós!

3

How Are You?

Draw a line from each English sentence to its Spanish translation.

Hello. How are you?   Me llamo Marta.

I am good.   Hola. ¿Cómo estás?

My name is Marta.   Me llamo Roberto.

What is your name?   ¿Cómo te llamas?

My name is Roberto.   Estoy bien.

Greetings

Write the English meaning next to the Spanish words below.
Find and circle the Spanish words.

Hola	Hello
Adiós	Goodbye
Buenos días	Good day
Buenas tardes	Good afternoon
Buenas noches	Good night
Hasta luego	See you later
Hasta mañana	See you tomorrow
Gracias	Thank you
De nada	You're welcome
Por favor	please
Sí	yes
No	no
Amiga	friend (female)
Amigo	friend (male)
Señor	Mr.
Señora	Mrs.
Señorita	Miss
señor	man
señora	woman
señorita	young woman

Puzzle Fun

Write the English meaning next to the Spanish words below.
Find and circle the Spanish words.

```
O U S E N O R I T A
H O L A M A P D A A
B B A M A S O E G N
U U M I N E R N R A
E E I I A N F B A S
N N G G N O A A C O
A A O A A R V E I M
S S E N D N O B I O
T N S E N O R I T E
A O S E N O R A N A
R C N A U A M I G A
D H G R A C I A S M
E E O D E N A D A R
S S A A D I O S A A
B U E N O S D I A S
```

hola _____

señorita _____ sí _____

adiós _____ no _____

buenas noches _____ amigo _____

gracias _____ buenas tardes _____

por favor _____ de nada _____

amiga _____ señora _____

señor_____ buenos días _____

My Family Is Special

My family is special. .... Mi familia es muy querida.

Let's learn how to say their names.....Aprendamos a decir sus nombres.

We call them.. .... Se llaman
    mother.................... madre
    father .... padre
    sister .... hermana
    brother .... hermano
    grandma .... abuela
    grandpa................. abuelo
    aunt .... tía
    uncle..................... tío

(Chorus 1:)

My family is special.................. Mi familia es muy querida.
We work and play together...... Trabajamos y jugamos juntos
and have fun........................... y nos divertimos.
My family is special. .... Mi familia es muy querida.
Laughing and learning,............. Riendo y aprendiendo,
growing together, ... creciendo juntos,
we're a team........................... somos un equipo.

We call them... .... Se llaman...
    mother.................... madre
    father .... padre
    sister .... hermana
    brother .... hermano
    grandma .... abuela
    grandpa................. abuelo
    aunt .... tía
    uncle..................... tío

(Chorus 1)

(Repeat names with Spanish words first.)

(Chorus 2:)

Mi familia es muy querida........ My family is special.
Trabajamos y jugamos juntos ... We work and play together
y nos divertimos .... and have fun.
Mi familia es muy querida........ My family is special.
Riendo y aprendiendo, ... Laughing and learning,
creciendo juntos,...................... growing together,
somos un equipo .... we're a team.

7

My Family

Draw a line between each Spanish word and the correct picture.
Write the English word for each Spanish word.

abuela

_____

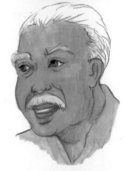

tía

_____

hermano

_____

padre

_____

abuelo

_____

My Family

tío

_____

madre

_____

hermana

_____

mi familia

_____

9

My Family Is Special

Write the Spanish word for each English word below.

mother _____

brother _____

grandpa _____

aunt _____

sister _____

father _____

grandma _____

Mini-Book Instructions: Make copies of the mini-book first, or carefully remove the pages to assemble. Cut each page along dashed line. Each story has eight pages. Place the pages in order. Staple the pages together along the left side to create the mini-book. Follow these instructions for each of the six mini-books throughout pages 11 – 48.

My Family
Mini-book

SONG — TRACK 4

Hello. My name is Sophie.
Hola. Mi nombre es Sofia.

This is my dog. His name is Thunder.
Este es mi perro. Su nombre es Trueno.

This is my brother. He likes to play baseball.
Este es mi hermano. A el le gusta jugar béisbol.

This is my baby sister. She likes her teddy bear.
Esta es mi hermanita. A ella le gusta su osito.

11

This is my mom. She likes to read books.

Esta es mi mamá. A ella le gusta leer libros.

This is my dad. He likes to watch television.

Este es mi papá. A el le gusta mirar televisión.

This is my grandma. She is a good cook.

Esta es mi abuela. Es muy buena cocinera.

This is my grandpa. He likes my grandma's cooking.

Este es mi abuelo. A el le gusta la comida de mi abuela.

This is my aunt. She brings me presents.

Esta es mi tía. Ella me trae regalos.

This is my uncle. He plays ball with us.

Este es mi tío. El juega a la pelota con nosotros.

This is my family.

Esta es mi familia.

We are celebrating my birthday.

Estamos celebrando mi cumpleaños.

6

These are my cousins.
Estos son mis primos.

We like to play outside.
Nos gusta jugar afuera.

8

mom...
...mamá

dad...
...papá

brother...
...hermano

baby sister...
...hermanita

grandma...
...abuela

grandpa...
...abuelo

uncle...
...tío

aunt...
...tía

my family...
...mi familia

Cousins...
...primos

Let's Eat

SONG
TRACK 5

We're sitting around waiting to eat. Grab your fork, come on, let's eat!
Estamos sentados esperando comer. Agarre tu tenedor, vamos, ¡a comer!

Please pass the...

chicken...............el pollo
potatoes ....las papas
carrots...............las zanahorias
bread................el pan
meat ....la carne
corn..................el maíz
rice....................el arroz
salad ....la ensalada
(Chorus)

Por favor pase...

el pollo...............chicken
las papas ....potatoes
las zanahorias .....carrots
el pan ....bread
la carne ....meat
el maíz..............corn
el arroz ....rice
la ensalada.........salad
(Chorus)

Please pass the...

fish ....el pescado
beans ....los frijoles
apples...............las manzanas
milk ....la leche
peas ....los guisantes
bananas............los plátanos
pie ....el pastel
cake ....la torta
(Chorus)

Por favor pase...

el pescado..........fish
los frijoles ....beans
las manzanas ......apples
la leche ....milk
los guisantes........peas
los plátanos........bananas
el pastel ....pie
la torta ....cake
(Chorus)

15

Foods

Circle the picture that shows the meaning of each Spanish word.

pollo

zanahorias

manzanas

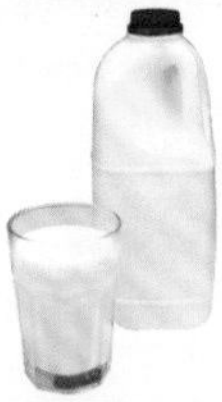

maíz

carne

ensalada

pan

papas

Word Scramble

Unscramble the following Spanish food words.

RAORZ

_____

ORTTE

_____

INGSTAESU

_____

NANASZAM

_____

OPNTLAÁS

_____

LOPLO

_____

PNA

_____

SJEROIFL

_____

MÍZA

_____

DLAASENA

_____

APEDSCO

_____

NRAEC

_____

PAASP

_____

LTEPAS

_____

ANASAZOIRH

_____

LHCEE

_____

Let's Eat

Answer the riddles. Write the correct Spanish food word.

People usually put dressing on me. **What am I?**

_____

If you like french fries, you like us. **What are we?**

_____

People drink me when they eat cookies. **What am I?**

_____

We are orange and grow in the ground. **What are we?**

_____

You usually use two slices of me when making a sandwich. **What am I?**

_____

We are small, green, and round. **What are we?**

_____

People like us in pies, as juice, or as a sauce. **What are we?**

_____

We can be green, black, brown, and even yellow. **What are we?**

_____

Word Bank

frijoles   ensalada

guisantes   zanahorias   pan

manzanas   leche   papas

SONG
TRACK 6

This is my grandma. She is a good cook.

Esta es mi abuela. Ella cocina muy bien.

My family likes to eat dinner together.

En mi familia nos gusta cenar juntos.

③

"I love the apple sauce, Grandma, " I say.

"Me gusta la salsa de manzana, abuela," digo yo.

"Thank you. Now eat some corn," says my grandma.

"Gracias. Ahora come un poco de maíz," dice mi abuela.

19

"Please pass the chicken and rice," my dad says.
"Por favor pasa el pollo y el arroz," dice mi papá.

"Please pass the salad," my mom says.
"Por favor pasa la ensalada," dice mi mamá.

"May I have some bread and butter?" asks my grandpa.
"¿Me dan un poco de pan y mantequilla?" pide a mi abuelo.

"Yes," says my grandma. "And here are some beans."
"Sí," dice mi abuela. "Y aquí hay frijoles."

"Please pass me the milk," says my brother.
"Por favor pásenme la leche," dice mi hermano.

"Here you go," my mom says.
"Aquí va," dice mi mamá.

"Of course I made dessert," says my grandma.
"Claro que preparé un postre," dice mi abuela.

"I made a great big chocolate cake!"
"¡Hice una gran torta de chocolate!"

"Did you make any dessert?" asks my dad.
"¿Preparaste un postre?" pregunta mi papá.

"Did you make any dessert?' asks my grandpa.
"¿Preparaste un postre?" pregunta mi abuelo.

chicken and rice...
...arroz con pollo

corn...
...maíz

bread and butter...
...pan y mantequilla

thank you...
...gracias

salad...
...ensalada

dessert...
...postre

beans...
...frijoles

chocolate cake...
...torta de chocolate

milk...
...leche

applesauce...
...salsa de manzana

The Five-Day Weather Forecast

SONG TRACK 7

What is the weather like today?
It is sunny.................................... Hace sol.

¿Qué tiempo hace hoy?
Hace sol.

What is the weather like today? ....
It is cloudy...................................

¿Qué tiempo hace hoy?
Está nublado.

What is the weather like today?
It is raining.................................

¿Qué tiempo hace hoy?
Está lloviendo.

What is the weather like today? ....
It is snowing.................................

¿Qué tiempo hace hoy?
Está nevando.

What is the weather like today?
It is cold...................................

¿Qué tiempo hace hoy?
Hace frío.

What is the weather like today?
It is hot ....

¿Qué tiempo hace hoy?
Hace calor.

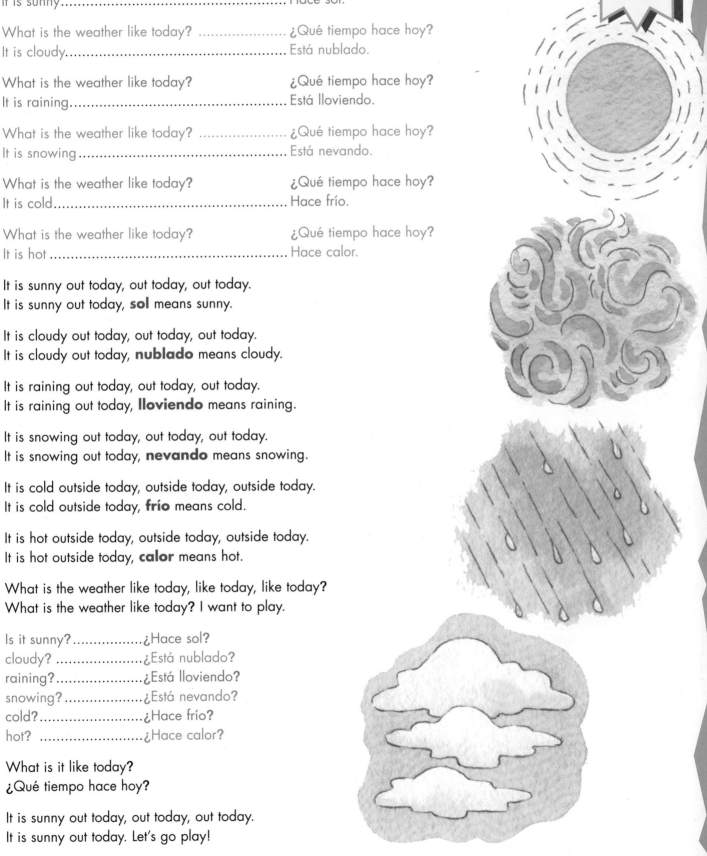

It is sunny out today, out today, out today.
It is sunny out today, **sol** means sunny.

It is cloudy out today, out today, out today.
It is cloudy out today, **nublado** means cloudy.

It is raining out today, out today, out today.
It is raining out today, **lloviendo** means raining.

It is snowing out today, out today, out today.
It is snowing out today, **nevando** means snowing.

It is cold outside today, outside today, outside today.
It is cold outside today, **frío** means cold.

It is hot outside today, outside today, outside today.
It is hot outside today, **calor** means hot.

What is the weather like today, like today, like today?
What is the weather like today? I want to play.

Is it sunny?.................¿Hace sol?
cloudy? ....¿Está nublado?
raining?....................¿Está lloviendo?
snowing? ....¿Está nevando?
cold?........................¿Hace frío?
hot? ....¿Hace calor?

What is it like today?
¿Qué tiempo hace hoy?

It is sunny out today, out today, out today.
It is sunny out today. Let's go play!

23

The Five-Day Weather Forecast

Look at the pictures. Write the correct Spanish phrase below on the line.

Está soleado   **Está nevando**   **Está nublado**

Hace frío   **Está lloviendo**   **Hace calor**

 _____

 _____

 _____

 _____

 _____

 _____

24

What Is The Weather Like Today?

Draw a line from the Spanish sentence to its English meaning.

Está soleado.	It is snowing.
Está nublado.	It is hot.
Está lloviendo.	It is cold.
Está nevando.	It is raining.
Hace frío.	It is sunny.
Hace calor.	It is cloudy.

25

Weather Fun

Draw a picture showing what the weather is like according to the Spanish sentence.

¿Qué tiempo hace hoy?
Hace sol.

¿Qué tiempo hace hoy?
Está lloviendo.

¿Qué tiempo hace hoy?
Está nublado.

¿Qué tiempo hace hoy?
Está nevando.

What is the Weather Like Today?
Mini-book

What is the weather like today?

¿Cómo está el tiempo hoy?

It is sunny.

Está soleado.

---

③

What is the weather like today?

¿Cómo está el tiempo hoy?

It is cloudy.

Está nublado.

What is the weather like today?

¿Cómo está el tiempo hoy?

It is hot.

Hace calor.

What is the weather like today?

¿Cómo está el tiempo hoy?

It is raining.

Está lloviendo.

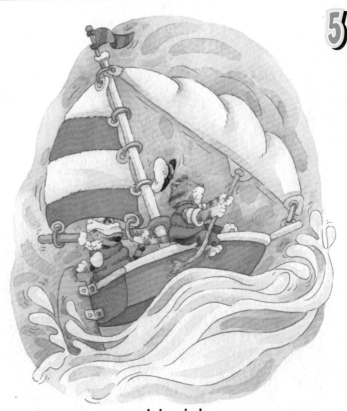

What is the weather like today?

¿Cómo está el tiempo hoy?

It is windy.

Hay viento.

What is the weather like today?

¿Cómo está el tiempo hoy?

It is cold.

Hace frío.

What is the weather like today?
¿Cómo está el tiempo hoy?

It is snowing.
Está nevando.

---

sunny...
...soleado

cloudy...
...nublado

It is hot...
...Hace calor

raining...
...lloviendo

windy...
...viento

snowing...
...nevando

cold...
...frío

today...
...hoy

weather...
...tiempo

What Should I Wear?

shirt.....................camisa
t-shirt ....camiseta
shorts ....pantalones cortos
pants ....pantalones
sweater..................suéter
skirt ....falda
underwear ....ropa interior
pajamas ....pijama
bathing suit ....traje de baño

socks ....calcetines
shoes.................zapatos
sandals ....sandalias

hat ....sombrero
gloves...................guantes
scarf....................bufanda
coat ....abrigo
raincoat ....impermeable
boots ....botas
umbrella ....paraguas

What Should I Wear?

Write the Spanish word for each item of clothing pictured.

_____   _____   _____

_____   _____   _____

_____   _____   _____

Word Bank

zapatos	abrigo	falda
botas	pantalones	pijama
suéter	camisa	camiseta

What Should I Wear?
Mini-book

Shirt, pants, socks, and shoes,
Camisa, pantalones, calcetines, y zapatos,

I put these on to go to school.
me los pongo para ir al colegio.

3

Sweater, skirt, necklace, and hat,
Suéter, falda, collar, y sombrero,

I put these on to go out to dinner.
me los pongo cuando salgo a cenar.

33

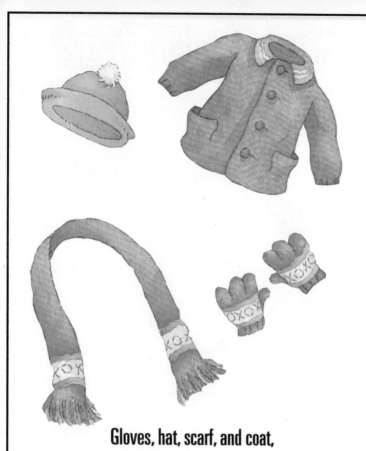

Gloves, hat, scarf, and coat,
Guantes, sombrero, bufanda y abrigo,

I put these on to go sledding.
me los pongo para ir en trineo.

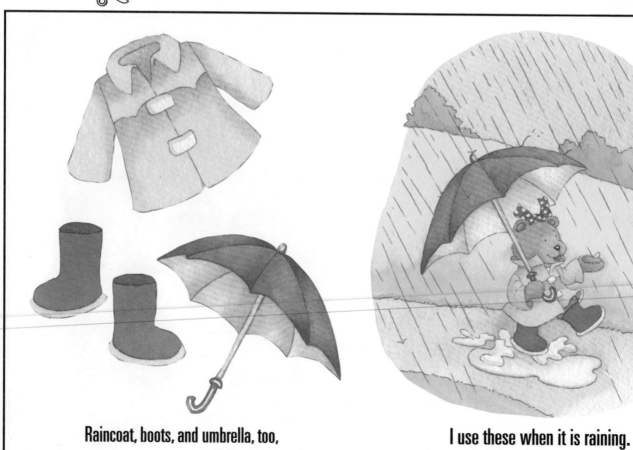

Raincoat, boots, and umbrella, too,
Impermeable, botas y un paraguas también,

I use these when it is raining.
los uso cuando está lloviendo.

Shorts, t-shirts, sandals, and sunglasses,
Pantalones cortos, camiseta,
sandalias, y lentes para sol,

I put these on when it is sunny.
me los pongo cuando hay sol.

Underwear, socks, pajamas, and teddy bear,
Ropa interior, calcetines, pijama, y osito,

That's all I need for bed. Goodnight.
Es todo lo que necesito para
ir a la cama. Buenas noches.

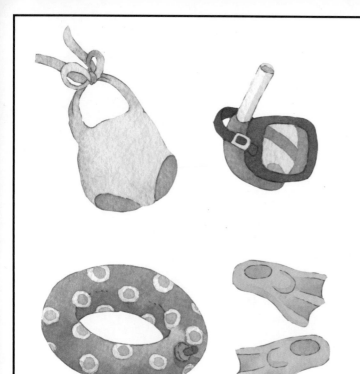

Bathing suit, goggles, flippers, and float,
Traje de baño, gafas para nadar, aletas, y flotador,

I use these to go swimming.
los uso cuando voy a nadar.

shirt...
...camisa

pajamas...
...pijama

shoes...
...zapatos

bathing suit...
...traje de baño

gloves...
...guantes

sandals...
...sandalias

umbrella...
...paraguas

skirt...
...falda

hat...
...sombrero

raincoat...
...impermeable

sweater...
...suéter

Learning Colors

We are going to teach you to pronounce each color name, and then we will sing a color song. Are you ready?

red	rojo
blue	azul
green	verde
yellow	amarillo
orange	anaranjado
purple	morado
pink	rosado
brown	café
black	negro
white	blanco

Great. Now let's say each color in Spanish, and then in English.

rojo	red
azul	blue
verde	green
amarillo	yellow
anaranjado	orange
morado	purple
rosado	pink
café	brown
negro	black
blanco	white

Red is rojo. Red is rojo.
Rojo is red. Rojo is red.
Learning all the colors is fun,
and colors are for everyone.
I like to shout and let you know
that red is rojo.

Blue is azul. Blue is azul.
Azul is blue. Azul is blue.
Learning all the colors is fun,
and colors are for everyone.
I like to shout and let you know
that blue is azul.

Green is verde. Green is verde.
Verde is green. Verde is green.
Learning all the colors is fun,
and colors are for everyone.
I like to shout and let you know
that green is verde.

Yellow is amarillo. Yellow is amarillo.
Amarillo is yellow. Amarillo is yellow.
Learning all the colors is fun,
and colors are for everyone.
I like to shout and let you know
that yellow is amarillo.

Orange is anaranjado.
Orange is anaranjado.
Anaranjado is orange.
Anaranjado is orange.
Learning all the colors is fun,
and colors are for everyone.
I like to shout and let you know
that orange is anaranjado.

Purple is morado. Purple is morado.
Morado is purple. Morado is purple.
Learning all the colors is fun,
and colors are for everyone.
I like to shout and let you know
that purple is morado.

Pink is rosado. Pink is rosado.
Rosado is pink. Rosado is pink.
Learning all the colors is fun,
and colors are for everyone.
I like to shout and let you know
that pink is rosado.

Brown is café. Brown is café.
Café is brown. Café is brown.
Learning all the colors is fun,
and colors are for everyone.
I like to shout and let you know
that brown is café.

Black is negro. Black is negro.
Negro is black. Negro is black.
Learning all the colors is fun,
and colors are for everyone.
I like to shout and let you know
that black is negro.

White is blanco. White is blanco.
Blanco is white. Blanco is white.
Learning all the colors is fun,
and colors are for everyone.
I like to shout and let you know
that white is blanco.

Learning Colors

In the crossword puzzle, write the Spanish color word that best describes each picture clue.

Across

3.

5.

7.

8.

9.

Down

1.

2.

4.

6.

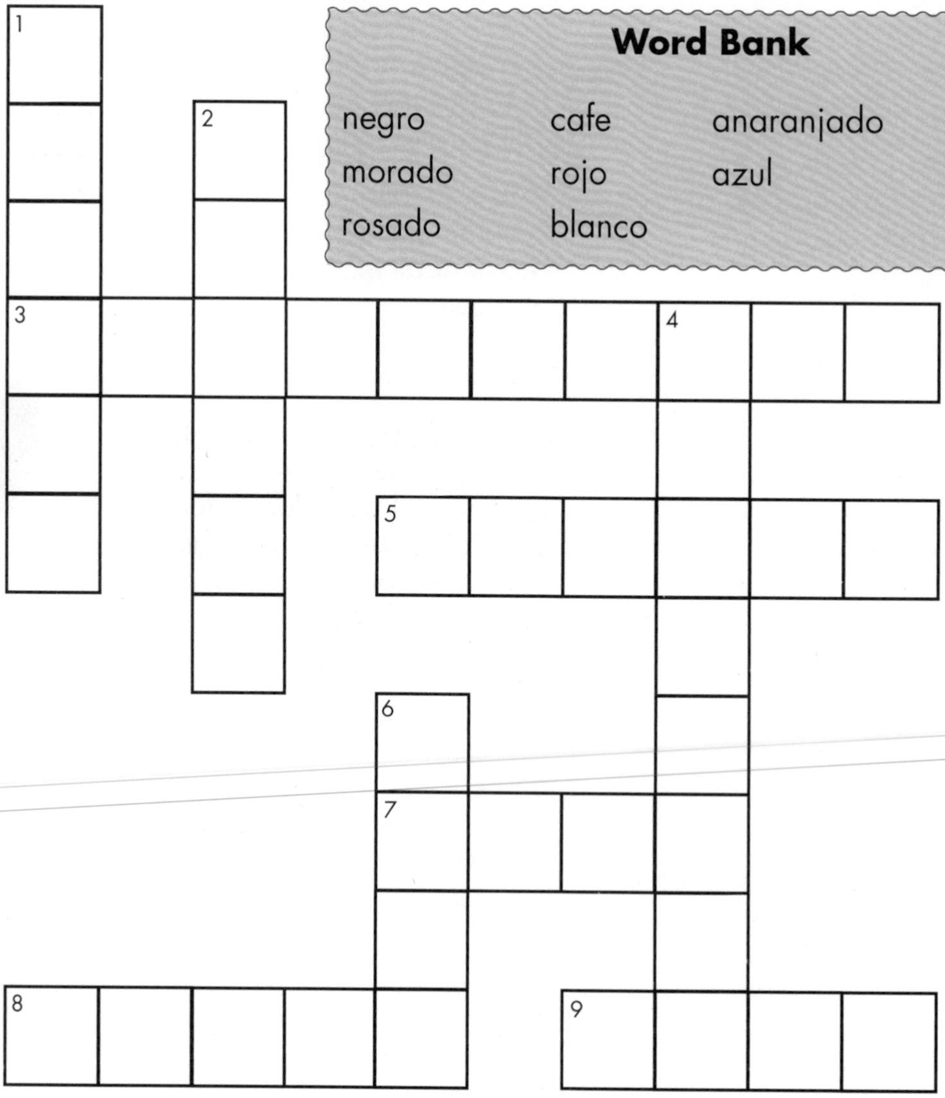

Word Bank

negro	cafe	anaranjado	verde
morado	rojo	azul	amarillo
rosado	blanco		

Green, Green Froggy
Mini-book

Verde,
verde
la ranita.

Verde, verde
la tortuga.

Verdes,
verdes
los guisantes.

Verdes,
verdes
las hojas.

Azul,
azul
el agua.

Azules,
azules
los pajaritos y

3

Azul,
azul
el cielo.

azul, azul el pastel.

39

Rojas, rojas
las manzanas.

Rojo, rojo
el color de la graciosa nariz del payaso.

Roja,
roja la rosa.

Amarilla,
amarilla la piña.

Amarillas, amarillas
las abejas jugando.

Amarillo,
amarillo el sol.

Moradas,

moradas las violetas.

Moradas,

moradas las uvas.

Moradas

las ciruelas que
me gusta probar.

He aprendido
los colores:

verde,

amarillo,

rojo,

morado,

y **azul,**

anaranjado,

y ya he terminado.

41

Anaranjadas,

anaranjadas las calabazas.

Anaranjadas,
anaranjadas
las zanahorias en mi platito.

Anaranjado,
anaranjado
el pez.

---

green... ...verde

purple... ...morado

red... ...rojo

orange... ...anaranjado

blue... ...azul

color... ...color

yellow... ...amarillo

colors... ...colores

How Do You Feel?

	femenino	**masculino**
happy	contenta	contento
sad	triste	triste
silly	tonta	tonto
mad	enojada	enojado
sick	enferma	enfermo
shy	tímida	tímido
embarrassed	avergonzada	avergonzado
surprised	sorprendida	sorprendido
tired	cansada	cansado
lonely	sola	solo
frightened	asustada	asustado

Sometimes I Feel

Draw a line between each Spanish word and the correct picture.

enojado

mad

triste

tired

cansada

sad

contenta

sick

enferma

happy

tímido

shy

Sometimes I Feel
Mini-book

SONG — TRACK 12

Sometimes I feel happy.

A veces me siento contenta.

Sometimes I feel sad.

A veces me siento triste.

Sometimes I feel sick.

A veces me siento enferma.

Sometimes I feel shy.

A veces me siento tímido.

Sometimes I feel silly.

A veces me siento tonta.

Sometimes I feel mad.

A veces me siento enojado.

Sometimes I feel embarrassed.

A veces me siento avergonzada.

Sometimes I feel surprised!

¡A veces me siento sorprendido!

Sometimes I feel tired.
A veces me siento cansada.

Sometimes I feel lonely.
A veces me siento solo.

No matter what I'm feeling, I know that it's okay
No importa cómo me sienta, sé que está bien

to have all kind of feelings each and every day.
tener todo tipo de sentimientos cada día.

Sometimes I feel frightened
A veces me siento asustada

and need a friend.
y necesito un amigo.

	FEMENINO	MASCULINO ⑧
happy...	...contenta	...contento
sad...	...triste	...triste
silly...	...tonta	...tonto
mad...	...enojada	...enojado
sick...	...enferma	...enfermo
shy...	...tímida	...tímido
embarrassed...	...avergonzada	...avergonzado
surprised...	...sorprendida	...sorprendido
tired...	...cansada	...cansado
lonely...	...sola	...solo
frightened...	...asustada	...asustado